In The Rarefied Regions of the Heart: Last Lines

In The Rarefied Regions of the Heart: Last Lines

Don Gutteridge

First Edition

Hidden Brook Press
www.HiddenBrookPress.com
writers@HiddenBrookPress.com

Copyright © 2020 Hidden Brook Press
Copyright © 2020 Author Name

All rights for poems revert to the author. All rights for book, layout and design remain with Hidden Brook Press. No part of this book may be reproduced except by a reviewer who may quote brief passages in a review. The use of any part of this publication reproduced, transmitted in any form or by any means, electronic, mechanical, photocopied, recorded or otherwise stored in a retrieval system without prior written consent of the publisher is an infringement of the copyright law.

In The Rarefied Regions of the Heart: Last Lines
by Don Gutteridge

Cover Design – Sol Terlson Kennedy
Layout and Design – Richard M. Grove

Typeset in Garamond
Printed and bound in Canada
Distributed in USA by Ingram, in Canada by Hidden Brook Distribution

Library and Archives Canada Cataloguing in Publication

Title: In the rarefied regions of the heart : last lines / Don Gutteridge.
Names: Gutteridge, Don, 1937- author.
Description: First edition.
        Poems.
Identifiers: Canadiana (print) 20200155296
        Canadiana (ebook) 2020015530X
        ISBN 9781927725986 (softcover)
        ISBN 9781927725993 (EPUB)
Classification: LCC PS8513.U85 I52 2020
        DDC C811/.54—dc23

For my grandson Tom.

Table of Contents

Loft – *p. 1*
Tactile – *p. 2*
Rudimentary – *p. 3*
Hallelujah – *p. 4*
Grail – *p. 5*
Brink – *p. 6*
Amity – *p. 7*
Chrysalid – *p. 8*
Tail Gunner – *p. 9*
Hilt – *p. 10*
Effortless – *p. 11*
Gait – *p. 12*
Stark – *p. 13*
Glazed – *p. 14*
Minstrelsy – *p. 15*
Pristine – *p. 16*
Tuft – *p. 17*
Pied – *p. 18*
Odds – *p. 19*
Horizon – *p. 20*
Conjunction – *p. 21*
Utterly – *p. 22*
Buoyancy – *p. 23*
Bower – *p. 24*
Lasalles – *p. 25*
Morning – *p. 26*
Reading the Runes – *p. 27*
Dazzle – *p. 28*
Innings – *p. 29*

Never Letting Go – *p. 30*
Then – *p. 31*
Young – *p. 32*
Awakening – *p. 33*
Ink – *p. 34*
Voluminous – *p. 35*
Anchor – *p. 36*
Music – *p. 37*
Enough – *p. 38*
Spangled – *p. 39*
Island – *p. 40*
Half Past – *p. 41*
Godspeed – *p. 42*
Anya – *p. 43*
Abide – *p. 44*
Alive – *p. 45*
Dream – *p. 46*
Monumental – *p. 47*
Bargain – *p. 48*

Fifteen for Anne
in loving memory

Aria – *p. 50*
Wave – *p. 51*
I Turned Away – *p. 52*
Choosing – *p. 53*
Allowed – *p. 54*
Smitten – *p. 55*
Souls – *p. 56*
Otherwise – *p. 57*
Embrace – *p. 58*

Voice – *p. 59*
I Miss You – *p. 60*
Unamazed – *p. 61*
Bath – *p. 62*
Chum – *p. 63*
Versifier – *p. 64*
Forsaken – *p. 65*
Friend – *p. 66*
One Summer – *p. 67*
Desire – *p. 68*
Everything Born – *p. 69*
Love – *p. 70*
Pied – *p. 71*
Pluck – *p. 72*
Breathing – *p. 73*
Hank – *p. 74*
Idaho – *p. 75*
Dreams – *p. 76*
Image – *p. 77*
Orpheus – *p. 78*
Surmise – *p. 79*
Assad – *p. 80*
Bounty – *p. 81*
The Wars – *p. 82*
Pinnacle – *p. 83*
Enchantment – *p. 84*
Simple – *p. 85*
Jaunty – *p. 86*
Match – *p. 87*
Succinct – *p. 88*
Aloud – *p. 89*
Matinėe – *p. 90*

Author Bio Notes – *p. 92*

Loft

How many a September morn
have I wakened to suns as yet
unborn, and tried
to remember the sea-soft
loft of my mother's womb
where it all began and where
a village awaited the abrupt
rupture of my arrival and, under
grandfather's hedge, hung
with lilacs, we sang the song
of my daylong being
and reveled in the lyric lustre
of our first words, flung
against the world's will.

Tactile
For John B. Lee

We wade bare-breasted
into Huron's chilled blue
waves and, breathing froth
as they crest and tumble into
themselves, they lick
at the shore-wide sand
like tactile tongues, and we feel
in the undulance of the undertow
the pull of moon-tugged
tides and the world's ruthless
will, and we dive in
anyway, content to be flung
afloat, to batten down
on buoyancy, to be fractured
by a June-juiced sun.

Rudimentary

And so it was hide-and-go-
seek under Mara's lamp
and a sky multitudinous
with stars where the moon loomed,
and we hid our secret selves
in shrouds of shadow, listening
only to the hum of our blood
and waiting for the "All Free!"
to come racing for home,
leaving behind something
raw. rudimentary, bruised
in the bone.

Hallelujah

When Shirley McCord was still
almost-a-woman, I willed
the bottle to spin her way
and was more than satisfied
at a winning smile, and later
in the day, jumping rope,
she raised her leg so high
I cried Hallelujah
and praised the Lord.

Grail

Nancy Mara was the first
girl I took a fancy to,
before I knew that love
was more than a quiver in the blood,
and I longed to be her Lancelot
going for the Grail and bringing
that cherished chalice home
to her, and how many a night
did I contrive at hide-
and-go-seek to huddle
next to her among the shivering
shadows, but when, with a surging
heart, I dared pledge my troth
no word emerged.

Brink

How many wintry evenings
did we spend night-skating
on Foster's Pond under
a cornucopia of stars
in an ink-dark sky
and a moon marooned in its own
glow, gliding in bonded
pairs like would-be,
fledgling lovers, sailing
as newly-minted sailors
to the very brink of the Earth's
edge.

Amity
For Shirley McCord, my childhood friend

Suddenly Shirley was more
than a girl, stirring in me
something alien, a buzzing
in the blood, a luffing of the
loins, and I knew even then
she would never again be
my buddy, that amorous amity
would never be enough.

Chrysalid

O the artful girls
of Canatara, unfurling
fresh-breasted upon
its glistening sands, and the bashful
boys of Canatara eye
them warily, beyond
the scope of hope, and the Heavenly
blue blaze of the Lake
and its leavening light ignite
something akin
to lust within their newly-
gendered, just-out-of-
the-chrysalid hearts, all
thought of tender contact
lost in the misfiring
of desire.

Tail Gunner

Jerry's Dad, the tail
gunner who survived five
seasons in a glass bubble
with bullets buzzing around him
like berserk bees, couldn't
drink enough booze
to muzzle the maelstrom
of his memories or the furlongs
of regurgitated fears, and his heart
simply hemorrhaged and Jerry
was bereft of the father he idolized,
while mine, who repaired the planes
that limped inland, wizened
in his son's eyes.

Hilt

Under a night-sky
quilted with stars we go
blading upon the moon-
glow glaze of Foster's
pond and in our feathered
weightlessness we flow
unshadowed a-gley,
free from the fixity of the
firmament, up to the hilt
in Heaven's gaze

Effortless

When Shirley McCord wasn't
tap-dancing (jittering
the sidewalk like a Bo
Jangles), she was twirling
her baton and strutting high-
thighed over Grandfather's
lawn like a drum majorette
in the Dominion Day parade
(her skirts a-whirl, effortlessly
eddying the air) and I marvelled
at the gumption of girls and the way
they moved to a music heard only
in the head.

Gait

Shirley and I prancing
through grandfather's whirl-i-
gig, its wrinkled spray
like a tantalizing tickle, and I try
not to gaze at her long-
legged gait and the way
her hair wimples in the wind
as she smiles with her eyes as if
to say, "Hurry up and wait,
girls are fickle."

Stark

Under Mara's lamp
and a stark sky engraved
with stars and the moon's looming
amplitude we ventured
into shapeless shadows shrouding
us from the unerring eye
of the one designated "It,"
and we huddled there witting
and waiting for the "All Free"
to ring through the vast void
of the shuddering firmament
and release us from the night terrors
plundering our blood.

Glazed

On the glazed globe of Leckie's
fallow, marinated by moon-
light, we skated free
of our everyday bodies,
our blades biting the ice
as precise as prisms, and Grace
and I, like a gendered pair,
striding side by side
and stroke for stroke as finely
tuned as Double Dutch)
our ungloved hands
barely a speck apart:
more tender than touch.

Minstrelsy

In Sunday School we sang
just to hear ourselves sing,
so loud the Reverend Buchanan's
jowls jiggled, our vigorous
vowels ringing the rafters
in jubilant song, all
the while hoping our sins
would be rescinded and that Heaven
would be moved by our minstrelsy.

Pristine

On our way to Canatara
we had to pass the Barker's
abode with its tar-papered
boards so cracked
the wind blew through them
and winter drifted in,
and in their back yard
the Barker kids, naked
as Adam, paddled listless
in the dirt, wishing it were green,
and I was so in love
with my own life I couldn't
give them a pinch of pity,
eager to reach our pristine
beach.

Tuft

That summer in Hendrie's
abandoned coop we played
"Show me your bum" (or send
me to the moon), and when
Joanne dropped her panties
I was mildly surprised at the
tuft between her thighs
(but chuffed enough to be randy)
until she grinned at mine
and, cock-a-hoop, said
"I didn't think they grew
them that tiny."

Pied

I was born with ink in my veins
and I teethed on grandfather's stories
of rambunctious bears and peregrinating
pigs who always came
in triplicate, and I don't remember
when I first heard a rhyme
chime, but something seethed
inside me, waiting to be
released, to be eased
in the pied precincts of a poem.

Odds

O the long-legged
girls of Canatara!
their curvilinear bodies
arrayed on the beach and squeezed
into their one-piece suits,
while those of the gentleman
gender lounge breezily
on the serpentine sands and reach
for the cusp of courage, larcenous
with lust, and weighing the odds.

Horizon

And once again we go
night-skating on Foster's
pond under a sky air-
brushed with stars and lacquered
by moonlight, where Nancy
Mara and I, her hand
folded in mine and stride
for stride, leave obsidian
meridians in our wake, knowing
that, for this bedizened
moment, no horizon
could hold us.

Conjunction

Where the dream begins and the village
ends lies the green
desmesne of the childhood
I stippled with stories and punctuated
with poems, and I was an emissary
from Eden, rinsed in innocence,
and since that day I have,
wielding words like a
drunken balladeer and singing
the song of myself, lived
my life at the conjunction of love
and belonging.

Utterly

Bill Barr's pool
room drew us to its
tantalizing temptations
like moths to a flicker of flame,
but, alas, a discreet curtain
marred out view of the dodgy
doings behind it, and we,
sipping our straw-drawn
Pepsis, were fated to be
mere listeners to the crisp
collision of ball and cue
or the feathered thunk in a far
pocket, and oh how we envied
the denizens inside and longed
for the day we would turn eighteen
and enter that satisfying sanctum
and be corrupted utterly.

Buoyancy

My pal Jerry swam
with the deft of a dolphin, while I
was left dog-paddling
in the shallows, dreaming of Johnny
Weismeuller and his Olympian
strokes, but we both loved
the lake that held us hallowed
in its blue buoyancy, and the grin
Jerry gave me reassured me
of my worth and the friendship
that buckled us together for all
the summer days of our boyhood
so we each faced the world,
enjoined by joy and the simplicities
of luck, saying aloud,
"Here I am."

Bower

The grass on grandfather's lawn
was as green as the leaves in Eden
and as I lay in its dandelion daze,
letting the sunlight lick me
lucid, I was undiminished
by the tyrannies of Time or the passing
of the hours, and I grew as elemental
as Adam in his pristine bower
and as innocent as Eve before
an apple intervened.

Lasalles

When I was young and my world
was new, we roamed the els
and alleyways of our village
like loose-limbed LaSalles
and our sun hung like a brass
medallion on the heft of its horizon
and we were as free-flung
as Adam in the echelons of Eden,
eschewing whatever threatened
to amputate our innocence and all
the while rhapsodizing on the
tonsured tillage of our town,
where every road led us
home.

Morning

How many times have I
in the morning of the world's awakening
found myself on Canatara's
silken sands amid its numinous
dunes with our Lake nearby,
older than the Attawandaron
who wandered there in Earth's
infancy to lay their faces
in its buoyant embrace while the
sun unfurled from the
heron-blue horizon like a
blown rose and I waited
under the hush of Heaven,
poised for poetry and is its bedizening
rhymes?

Reading the Runes

These dunes, soothing
the shores of Canatara,
are older than Adam extant
or Eve un-ribbed,
and Coop and I lie
on their sun-strummed sand
while the heat of a hundred centuries
roves in our bones and hums
in our blood, and Coop says
with his deliberate grin, "Let's
cool off!" and we dove
into the elemental cold
of our Lake like Baptists seized
ecstatic and reading the runes.

Dazzle

Hollyhocks batten
down on frazzled barn-
boards all over the town
I was born to, hemorrhaging
hues of every ilk,
and the morning sun, as satin
as silk, sweetens the petticoated
petals the girls metamorphose
into ballroom gowns
or prom-night frocks,
while I, in the island of my
innocence, drown in their dazzle.

Innings

September was the season of misted
meadows, of stoked sheaves
sweetened by the sun, of the glacial
glide of Holsteins grazing
Leckie's pristine pastures,
of a gravel road gilded
with goldenrod and down which
we travelled to our one-room
country school, and the girls
at a startle of starlings cried
"My wedding!" and the boys eyed
the chestnut stallion
Gracie would ride with her scissoring
thighs, and we had the sense
of a world just beginning
where it was our innings.

Never Letting Go

When I was barely alive,
my mother took me by the hand
and walked me through grandfather's
milkweed meadow,
its blooms inking the air
pink, and I unhatched
a wizened pod just
to watch the fluff silken
the breeze above my lionizing
eyes, and monarchs
with two moons on their butterfly
bodies fluttered and lit
on the drooping leaves, and on
we meandered, my mother,
unamazed, leading the way,
me in tow, never
letting go.

Then

I was enwombed by a village
and I felt as safe within
its green demesnes as Adam
in the dappled dells of Eden,
and had no need to venture
to the volatile verges where the Other
lurked like Eve's uneaten
apple, and everything wondrous
had a name I envowelled, a flexible
lexicon I would deploy
in the inked precincts of a poem,
and I prayed I would stay in those
uncontaminated confines
from then until Doomsday.

Young

Mara's lamp hung
over the indelible dark
of Monk Street like a
tide-tugging moon,
and under the inked blinking
of stars in the high dome
of the sky we played hide-
and-go-seek (one of us
"It" the others scampering
for the post like jittering
juggernauts) and we were
young enough not
to care what lay beyond
the amplitude of Mara's
numinous light, so
free and chuffed were we,
gamboling in the lunar glow,
our hearts heightened, hugged
by home.

Awakening

The sun rises over
First Bush, the lava
of its light like the slow
opening of a June rose,
lacquering the leafage
and rousting robins from their
yellow-beaked sleep,
setting butterflies a-flutter
in the breath of a breeze and then
anointing a village by a Lake
with its lucid layering before
seeping agleam into alleys
and ells, and there on a
sun-strummed street
stands a boy something
like me, navigating the day's
breaking, a-dream with desire,
waiting once again
for the world's awakening.

Ink

When I was just alive
a village awaited my robust
arrival and together we stencilled
our joint story in a thousand
petrified poems about sunrises
over First Bush, the soft-
sung sands of Canatara,
the ebullient blue of our resident
Lake, the rattle of cattails
in Foster's Pond, the Pickwickian
characters the Point was peopled with,
the green ease of Grandfather's
lawn and the room above it
where I was unwombed,
blinking ink.

Voluminous

The day my grandmother died
the lilacs in our yard bloomed
voluminous, and I felt like an infant
ripped from a womb and wondered
whether the seasons would find
again their ritual rhythms
and ease my bereavement,
but May flowed into June
and buds blossomed in the throes
of my loss, and I prayed that something other than my grief
would abide.

Anchor

And so we go a-kiting
on the wind-weathered Flats,
our Tiger Moths bulging
in the big-bellied breeze
off the Lake, tethered
fast in our fists, and we spool
out our lines inch
by inch and our taut rigs
hesitate and thither, bank
and surprise, feathering
a froth of cloud where the sun
sits in the noon-daze
and the moon silvers a far
horizon and we dream of Icarus
unwinched from Earth's anchor.

Music

In the beginning was the birth of the word
that blossomed in my blood and moved
like a metaphor of the Earth and me
and I was born stuttering stanzas,
lost in the glossary of syllables
that sang me felicitous and I found
my home in the prism of a poem
and in the village that wound me
willing into its emerald embrace
and together we storied the ground
with passions and plots that took
the sheen off of Eden and shook
loose the music of the Muses.

Enough

And me pencilling my first
saga: Bill Breckinridge,
Boy Detective, and how
puffed with pride I was
when the school scribbler
with the glazed covers was full
of the words I'd spun out of
my unbibbed imagination,
and little did I know, between
jolts of joy, that in the
henceforth days
I would continue to confect
plots and paradigms, waiting
for the amazed world to cry
"Hold! Enough!"

Spangled

Dad and I angling
on Mitchell's Bay, me
in awe of his "wobbler" brushing
the surface with a limpid dimple
and the slow tease of the lure
and the big pike's barracuda
bite and the easing out
of the line with just enough
play in it and Dad's eyes
alight with unsurprise
as I net our catch and let
his grin flow over me,
soothing and spangled.

Island

They called it a subdivision,
but Orchard Park was our home
ground (even though
the apple trees were cut down
to make room for our houses
and the land was pancake flat)
and we were hugged by farmers
fields and daisy-dotted
meadows, and we lived as true
and upright as any village
where neighbours grew in communal
felicity, sitting cozily
on their porches, watching the world
whirl by, where road-hockey
games under bright lights
echoed cheerily and baseball
games saw boys of every
ilk and hue play
in harmony's embrace until
the gloaming gathered them in,
where we, islanded in our innocence,
felt the tug of the place
we loved.

Half Past

When we pass on, part
 our language goes with us:
my grandmother always said:
"Don't be a fuss budget,"
or more quaintly "It's
half past four,"
keeping the latter phrase
alive while the digital age
has made it moribund, but
whenever I think of Gran,
long gone to her grave,
I look at the kitchen clock
and say, "Half past five."

Godspeed
For Tom

You tell me you are planning
to move to the wide, abiding
spaces of Idaho to nurture
dairy cows and be
a companion to your inamorata,
and I am more than happy
to lose you to such felicity
and hope your life has a fairy-
tail ending, for I have known you
since that day when you,
blue-eyed in your incubator,
said howdy to the world,
and I wish you nothing but
Godspeed.

Anya

O how we loved your frantic
antics, the way you greeted
everybody at the door
like an enthusiastic butler,
the tricks you learned just
to please your puzzling patrons,
the deep well of tail-
wagging affection you gave
with such a generous joy,
and we will miss you long
after the echo of your presence
has faded.

Abide

I wake and feel the weight
of the dark and realize you are
no longer sleeping
beside me, but I am comforted
by the thought of stars startling
and the moon's balloon pillowing
a hushed horizon, and I
must learn to bestill
an aching heart, bear
what the world has brought me,
and abide.

Alive

For my Uncle Potsy in memoriam

Saturday afternoon
on Cameron, anchored in the
off-shore reeds
and the second it starts to rain
the fish begin to bite
like barracudas and soon
it is a feeding frenzy
and the bottom of Ernie Rosenbloom's
row-boat is a mass
of squirming perch and I catch
my uncle's eye and the twinkle
there is as deep as our ink-
dark Lake (where the big
bass thrive) and I feel it
in the throes of my bones, dancing
cadenzas for the just-joy
of being alive.

Dream

You interrupt my dream of you
in all your lyrical loveliness,
and I am doubly blessed,
having you in the sweet desmesnes
of my sleep then again
when I wake to celebrate the miracle
of our coupled love.

Monumental

For Bob in loving memory

Listening to Tchaikovsky's "Pathetique"
and its sonorous serenities, I am
reminded of you and how much
you loved those classics,
drowning in their decibels, feeling
the tremor of a tympani in the brevity
of your bone, the soaring of violins
in the gist of your blood, and O
how I regret all the years
we grew apart and how happy
I was when we came together
as brothers bred so you
could die and I could mourn
your passing and know that I
could always find you again
in this monumental music.

Bargain

We agreed that I would go
first, burning out
at forty like Dylan, and you,
as happy as a hippo in a
soothing slough, would live
to mourn my premature passing,
but alas you broke our bargain,
and my heart.

THIRTEEN FOR ANNE
in loving memory

Aria

Outside my window the oriole's
aria pierces the air
with melodious ease, and some-
where just beyond
the breeze's breath a mourning
dove throbs, and I am reminded
how much you loved such
ornithological music,
and something softens
in my soul and I am no
longer alone with my grief.

Wave

For fifty-seven years
we rode the same wave
and if it was not always
smooth sailing, we weathered
together whatever storms
torqued our horizons, and as
the Earth grew moonward
our love bloomed like a
June rose softened
by sunlight, and when you left
with no goodbyes and no
heroics, my heart was a coffined
candle pruned to the wick.

I Turned Away

I turned away for an immeasurable
moment and you were gone,
slipping serenely into silence
as if to say, "I didn't wish
to disturb," and I treasure
such thoughtfulness,
borne as it was out of
the long years of our loving
face to face, and I hope
when I make my peace I'll go
home with the quiet grace
of your leaving.

Choosing

O how you loved "Power
and Politics" for you were the
original news junky
(a debunker of bunkum)
because you knew we were not
put on this Earth to be
alone, that love was something
to be shared, something
that flowered in our souls and kept us
bound neighbour to neighbour,
and losing you has left me halved
but, above all, choosing
to live as you did, caring
as best as I can.

Allowed

O how you loved your Puccini
and his La Boheme with its sopranos
soaring to high C and a tenor
trumpeting his lungs aloud
over Mimi dying of TB
in a Paris garret, and after
a Chianti or two we'd put on
that groove-worn LP
and drown ourselves in the succulence
of sound until the sheen
of the tears we shed together
moved us as close as any
two souls are allowed.

Smitten

Eve may have bitten the apple
and lost Paradise, but I
for one applaud her gumption,
her thirsting after knowledge
of love's gaudy grapple,
its rich itch, and you
were one of her daughters, first
in my eyes, and I would give up
a dozen dappled Edens
to be smitten by you
one more time.

Souls

I wake and delve the dark
in search of the last lingering
whisper of a dream in which
you smiled as if to say,
"I am still alive somewhere,
so let us be ourselves,
clasp hands like a pair
of day-breaking lovers,
and ask our souls to sing."

Otherwise

These hawks (a mated
pair?) ride the up-
drafts in a sky as blue
as my darling's eyes, and I
think of you now, watching
these birds, coupled
for life, winging their way
through the rarefied air,
rocking on the breeze's
billow, and it would be
sacrilege to wish the world,
without you, were otherwise.

Embrace

It's hard to believe that almost
a year has passed since you took
your leave, and though I am
no longer hobbled by the grip
of grief, my sadness suddens
whenever I see your face
in the mists of my mind or hear
your voice echoing inside,
ever soft and low like Lear's
Cordelia, and I wish I had
the Bard's touch to say
what still throbs in the shards
of my heart (knowing you would
widen your smile whatever
words I could confect
and beguile me once again
as you did when the world in its
amorous embrace, willed us
to never part.)

Voice

O how I long to have you
here once more, coming
back like grandfather's
lilacs, lacquered with light,
heralding Earth's rebirth
or like the slow explosion
of bulb and bloom, bevelling
the ground's glove, soliciting
sun, but nothing returns
from the darkness you have been dealt
and not even love can make you
whole again, and though
I listen hard for your voice
from some veiled vista,
all I can hear is the crack
of a Doomsday gun.

I Miss You

I miss you in the morning
when roses surrender to the sun,
I miss you at the nub of noon
when lilacs, steeped in light,
are tender to the touch,
I miss you in the amber afternoon
when meadows bloom with such delight,
I miss you in the evening
when day goes down with the breeze's
breath, and most of all
I miss you at night when our mutual
room is shorn of your shadow
and I am left alone, heart-heavy
and bitter to the bone.

Unamazed

O how you loved a jigsaw!
your ardent eye appraising
the thousand pieces sprawled
higgledy-piggledy on the table
below, and like a cartographer
with a sextant you drew the swerves
and bevels in your mind before
exacting them in place until,
like Van Gogh brushstrokes
the scene slowly shaped
itself and you sighed with un-
amazed satisfaction.

Bath

O how you loved your bath
(you were always half amphibian)
and the lolling languor of Rubenesque
ripples in that womb-warm
sea, liberated by nudity
in a room all your own,
and how I wish I could hear
again the gushed rush
of tap-water and the soft
sigh you utter as you submerge
like a serene submarine,
and know that I am no longer
alone.

Chum
For Shirley McCord

The next time I saw Shirley
she was curled on the svelte pelt
of Canatara's sands
and in the interim she grew
brand-new curves
and coombs in the first bloom
of her womanhood and a one-
piece suit that clung
like sifted silk and left me
tongue-tied, blissfully
vexed, benumbed
by a girl I once called
"chum."

Versifier

When god blew Adam out of
Eden's dust, He said,
"You must name all the things
I have provided thee,"
and Adam felt his tongue
torque about something
that became word he heard
himself say "This be a rose,"
and "This a tulip," and Eve,
recently unzipped
from a rib, asked, "What
be these?" and Adam,
searching for the word's
first idea, said "These
be flowers," and, enchanted
by his petal-perfect bower,
added, "You are my red,
red rose, my blood-
blooming tulip," and Eve
knew that Beauty had been
embodied in such similes
and that Adam was God's versifier

Forsaken

For Oscar Martinez and his daughter
After an image shown on TV

You lie there on the weeping banks
of the Rio Grande as if
feigning sleep, as if
you had drifted there from a dream
of a better life on the other
side, a father's arms
folded lovingly over a daughter
who will never see freedom
from the grip of murderous
gangs or soul-shrivelling
poverty, and I wonder when
the world will waken and images
like this will rupture our hardened
hearts and the hopes of Oscar
and his dead daughter will not
be forsaken again.

Friend
For Alvin Gehl

You were the one who consoled
a friend weeping for a lost
cause, who put a brotherly
arm around Stewart Warner
when the epilepsy seized him
and guided him safely home
and who made sure wee Sandy
Hales got picked first
for move-up, and you
remind me over the phone-
line connecting our sixty-
year separation that I once
stayed the night at your place
and hogged the pillow, and I try
my best to recall that youthful
intimacy, grateful that our lives
have been enmeshed with memories.

One Summer

For Sandra Grocott Gamble

Your hand folded in mine,
we made a bold promenade
along the sidewalks of our home
terrain, all eyes
lingering on your loveliness, and I
was as proud as a peacock
in its plumage, and even though
love bloomed but briefly
for one singular summer,
fading with autumn's languishing
leaves, I remember it still,
almost eighty years on,
feel it still singing
inside.

Desire

I listen to Crystal singing
"Running Away Down
River Road" and I have
such a longing to be
back where I began
and begin again, both
feet touching the home
ground, bound to its ballast
by the blood of belonging, and I yearn
to re-live those years
with all their pain and pleasure,
to burn with the unmuzzling
desire to be what I once
was.

Everything Born

When Eve ambushed the apple,
she swapped Eden for a world
where everything born must die
but not before the first
bloom-burst, before the fecund
fuse of procreation in the Earth's
renewable womb, before the sizzle
of sex and the breech-birth
of poetry to assuage and condole,
and I for one cheered
her cheek, grateful for every
breath I draw that denies
for a day my inexorable end
and leaves me living and wielding
words to celebrate that dappled
garden and Eve's spiteful
bite.

Love

When Eve upset Eden's
applecart, she found
herself rudely nude
before Adam grappling
with sudden sight and who,
ever the gentleman, passed her
a fig leaf to camouflage
her furred furrow,
as she giggled at the dozen
new delights and, no thanks
to the One Above, they soon
discovered what love was.

Pied

I was born with ink in my veins
and I teethed on grandfather's stories
of rambunctious bears and peregrinating
pigs who always came
in triplicate, and I don't remember
when I first heard a rhyme
chime, but something seethed
inside me, waiting to be
released, to be eased
in the pied precincts of a poem.

Pluck

And once again it is you,
Loretta, filling my cloistered
room with the lyrical loft
of your unforgettable voice,
and I dream you in the green
desmesnes of your cabin'd home,
barefoot in the sun-softened
grasses, a song rising
like a robin's throb in your throat,
grooming yourself for stardom
and letting me drown in the rustic
majesty of your music until all
I can hear is the unhobbled
grace-note of your Kentucky
pluck.

Breathing

Whenever I think upon
my demise, I try to remember
that mystical moment when I was
welcomed into my mother's womb
and sang in that sea-soft
solution until my abrupt eruption
into the world's room, uttering
a cry like a one-word
stanza that I would spin
into stories and ambling iambics,
and know that when my eyes
close for the final time
some part of me will still
be breathing.

Hank

It begins with a hum in your bones,
becomes a thrum in the throat
and utters itself in a song
you give to the world just
for the joy of it, and you sing
of unrequited love, the flutter
of lust and the ache of the
aloneness you felt as a fatherless
boy, and I see you still,
spinning your hillbilly magic
at the Grand Old Op'ry
or driving from country burg
to country burg, where even
the whiskey couldn't depose
the demons that rose through
your lacerating lyrics, until
the morphine and booze left you
comatose in your Cadillac,
redeemed at last in an indignant
death.

Idaho

For Tom

The more we age the more
we say Goodbye than Hello,
and now you tell me you're off
to America to abide with your
inamorata, and I picture
prairies rolling with wheat,
foothills wild
with horses and deserts steamed
with heat, and I see you,
having turned life's page,
strolling with your girl across
the sun-softened, dream-
drenched meadows of Idaho.

Dreams
For Kate

You came out feet-first
as if you wanted the world
to take note of your arresting
arrival, and when you turned
your eyes my way, bright
as beryl, full of un-
surprise and bringing news
from the womb, my heart
burst at the seams and love
burned through me like a slow
fuse, and I knew even then
we would spend a lifetime
sharing dreams.

Image

For my grandsons, Tim and James

In this cherished photo
you are sprawled on a plush sofa
like a pair of Rubenesque nudes,
blue-eyed and brown,
your impish grins alight
with the simple innocence of being
too young to know better,
and each time I turn
the image over in my lettered
hand, seeing it anew,
I feel a rush of love
in the rarefied region of my heart
that will last as long as I do.

Orpheus
For Tom

O how like Orpheus
you were, with your harp-strummed
melodies that becalmed the beasts
of the field, and you've always had
a touch of the horse-whisperer
in you and, unlike
that myth-man, you never
looked back, never yielded
to any tune but the one
humming in your head, and we loved you
with such unflinching
force that no music,
celestial or otherwise,
can ever diminish it

Surmise

We couldn't afford a photographer
to make a fancy portrait
of bride and groom, all
I have is a fading black-
and-white image, where we
stand a-tiptoe,
nose to nose the better
to see the surmise in the other's
eyes: that our love was more
roseate than mere romance.

Assad

Even the beasts of the field
do not torture or maim:
the lioness dispatches her prey
with a grateful snap of the neck,
the wolf has a taste for the jugular
and the Great White shreds
its victim with a single bite
(even the kitten, too
long domesticated, toys
with its mouse no more
than a moment), but you, Assad,
a-lust with power, poison
your own people with mustard
and watch as they hug death,
and it will take a thousand
thousand dawns before
another comes out of the womb
like you, who bring new meaning
to the word "monster."

Bounty

When the wind breathes on the wheat
and sun seethes in the corn,
the Earth gives up her bounty
and I think of our forebears
so long ago
in faraway counties
in the morning of a new world
truncating trees and sowing
oats by hand between
the charred stumps and watching
the furrows greening in the
summer's heat, and O
how I admire their gumption,
their unremitting toil,
the sweetness of their sweat as they
inadvertently planted
a land.

The Wars

My grandfather suffered three
years in the war to end
wars, where life expectancy
was eight weeks – amid
the stilted stutter of machine-
guns and shells that burst
like blown roses and mustard
gas, larcenous in the lungs,
and mud-mire in the trenches,
and it took more than a kind
of courage and more than hope
wilting in the Flanders rain
to dream of home where a woman
waited, still stunned
by love.

Pinnacle

Once again I dream you
into being, feel your breath
upon my face, take your hand
and stroll with you once more
on the Doon Pinnacle, where something
grand and giving took place
and, seeing you there beneath
a June moon and under
a parasol of stars, I think
that Beauty is God's embodiment
and Love its intimate twin.

Enchantment
For Anne in loving memory

How often we took for granted
the soaring of that first
enchantment, when we were young
enough to welcome the world
and all that awaited, and our leavening
love was a song on the sweet
ellipsis of your lips, and I wanted
only to compose poems
so perfect they would burst alive
between us and the words of my roaring
could be heard as high as the Heavens.

Simple

How many times on Sunday
mornings did I watch
my grandmother dimpling
dough for half-a-dozen
pies, rolling it wafer-
thin, crimping the edges
 before sugaring the spies
(while her better cousins
were off to church to sanctify
their sins) knowing there many
ways to love thy neighbour,
and that even simple acts
might be blessed in God's eyes.

Jaunty
For Judy Hammond and CCI

They rush from the girl's gym
onto the lush lawn
of our playing field, long
legs scissoring seductively
in the sun, while we watch
from afar, our senses jarred jaunty
(and wishing we had the pluck
to try our luck.)

Match

My Uncle Tom and I
loved our golf, meandering,
in linked tandem, meadowed
fairways as green as the desmenes
of Eden, and his drives sweetened
the summer's breeze and his wedges
softened the ball aloft
before it settled an inch
from the pin, and I smiled
as he grinned and sunk the putt,
and I think often of those
amiable afternoons, in sunshine
or rain, and that day,
when striving to win a match
that didn't matter, his heart
shattered like a window pane.

Succinct

Like the Bard, I tried
never to blot a line.
let the ink dry on the page,
for sonnets must have their rhyme,
ballads their beat and haiku
their views, and fiction
without a plot goes askew,
and so it is I look
my Muse straight in the eye
and give her a succinct wink.

Aloud

And there I was all
a-tingle on Gran's verandah,
reading aloud my first
story (deftly transcribed
in my school scribbler as the)
Adventures of Little Tiny
Bingo) to an audience of two,
pausing every now
and then for dramatic effect,
and after the last unslurred
word, I waited in vain
for glory, or applause.

Matinée

At our Saturday matinée
the hero always wore black
and rode a white horse
(with a nickering neigh) into a
sagebrush saga
and cartoon villains died
bloodlessly for our amusement,
and Cochise, the only good
Indian allowed by the Hollywood
henchmen with a penchant for powwows,
shunned the war-dance
for the pipe of peace, and these
were the stories that fuelled my fancy,
and magnified my imagination,
that I spun into a cornucopia
of tales and poems peppering
the page for seven decades.

Don Gutteridge lives in London, Ontario, was born in Sarnia and raised in the nearby village of Point Edward. He taught High School English for seven years, later becoming a Professor in the Faculty of Education at Western University, where he is now Professor Emeritus.

He is the author of seventy books: poetry, fiction and scholarly works in educational theory and practice. He has published twenty-two novels, including the twelve-volume Marc Edwards mystery series, and thirty-seven books of poetry, one of which, *Coppermine*, was short-listed for the 1973 Governor-General's Award. In 1970 he won the UWO President's Medal for the best periodical poem of that year, "Death at Quebec."

To listen to interviews with the author, go to:
http://thereandthen.podbean.com.

Fiction:

Bus-Ride. Nairn publishing: Nairn, 1974.
All in Good Time. Black Moss: Windsor, 1980.
St. Vitus Dance. Drumlin: London, 1986.
Shaman's Ground. Drumlin: London, 1988.
How the World Began. Moonstone: Goderich, 1991.
Summer's Idyll. Oberon: Ottawa, 1993.
Winter's Descent. Oberon: Ottawa, 1996.
Bewilderment. Borealis: Ottawa, 2000.
The Perilous Journey of Gavin the Great. Borealis Press: Ottawa, 2010.
The Rebellion Mysteries. Simon and Schuster: Toronto, 2012.
Lily's Story.(e-book). Bev Editions: Toronto, 2013 (Print edition 2014)
Constable Garrett and the Dead Ringer. Tellwell: Victoria, 2016
Lily Fairchild, Tablo publications, 2019.

Marc Edwards Mysteries:

Turncoat. McClelland and Stewart: Toronto, 2003.
Solemn Vows. McClelland and Stewart: Toronto, 2003.
Vital Secrets. Trinity: Saint John, 2007.
Dubious Allegiance. Simon and Schuster: Toronto, 2012.
Bloody Relations. Simon and Schuster: Toronto, 2013.
Death of a Patriot. Simon and Schuster: Toronto, 2014.
The Bishop's Pawn. Bev Editions: Toronto, 2015. (only e-book)
Desperate Acts. Bev Editions: Toronto, 2015. (only e-book)
Unholy Alliance. Bev Editions: Toronto, 2015. (only e-book)
Minor Corruption. Bev Editions: Toronto, 2015. (only e-book)
Governing Passion. Bev Editions: Toronto, 2015. (only e-book)
The Widow's Demise. Bev Editions: Toronto, 2015. (only e-book)

Don Gutteridge has had **37 books of poetry** published including his most recent, Hidden Brook Press, books: *Home Ground* – 2018, *Village Dreaming* – 2019, *The Star-Brushed Horizon* – 2019, *Out of the Blue* – 2019, *Inking the World* – 2019, *The Rarefied Regions of the Heart: Last Lines* – 2020, followed by his, over 600 page collected works, entitled; *Point Taken* – 2020.

www.ingramcontent.com/pod-product-compliance
Lightning Source LLC
Chambersburg PA
CBHW022011120526
44592CB00034B/782